SIT & SOLVE®

Brain-Boosting IQ Tests

Fraser Simpson

PUZZLE
WRIGHT
PRESS

An imprint of Sterling
Publishing Co., Inc.

www.puzzlewright.com

Puzzlewright Press, the distinctive Puzzlewright Press logo, and Sit & Solve
are registered trademarks of Sterling Publishing Co., Inc.

2   4   6   8   10   9   7   5   3   1

Published in 2010 by Sterling Publishing Co., Inc.
387 Park Avenue South, New York, NY 10016
© 2003 by Fraser Simpson
Originally published under the title *Sit & Solve IQ Tests*
Distributed in Canada by Sterling Publishing
%/o Canadian Manda Group, 165 Dufferin Street
Toronto, Ontario, Canada M6K 3H6
Distributed in the United Kingdom by GMC Distribution Services
Castle Place, 166 High Street, Lewes, East Sussex, England BN7 1XU
Distributed in Australia by Capricorn Link (Australia) Pty. Ltd.
P.O. Box 704, Windsor, NSW 2756, Australia

Printed in China
All rights reserved

Sterling ISBN 978-1-4027-7499-7

For information about custom editions, special sales, premium and
corporate purchases, please contact Sterling Special Sales
Department at 800-805-5489 or specialsales@sterlingpublishing.com.

Contents

Test 1

1. Which anagram is the odd one out?

INCH KEEN EARTH FRINGE SATCHMO THRONE

2. What do saddles, orchestras, and rhinos have in common?

3. The same pair of letters can be inserted side-by-side into each of the four words below, forming a new word each time. What pair of letters is it?

PARIS

IRATE

MOREL

FRIES

4. A cardboard box measuring 7 by 14 by 5 is filled full with 1 by 1 by 1 sugar cubes. How many of these 490 sugar cubes touch the box with at least one face?

5. A 7-letter landing spot is formed by taking a 3-letter body part above the shoulders and putting it inside a 4-letter body part, also found above the shoulders. What's the 7-letter landing spot?

6. Insert the 18 exterior letters into the grid to form a word square with words reading across and down. Each letter must be inserted into the same row or column that it is beside. All of the exterior letters will be used once each.

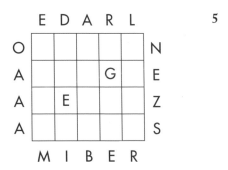

7. What is the next term in the following sequence?

6   14   30   62   126   254   _____

8. Insert the name of a tree into each set of blanks to make longer words.

CL _ _ _ ROOM   H _ _ _ ET

E _ _ _ ITNESS   DO _ _ _ _ SS

ABE _ _ _ _ _ IAN   INFI _ _ _ _ _

9. If you phonetically remove the first sound of BANKER, you hear ANCHOR. What word for an orchestral instrument sounds like something you might find in an orchestra member's hand when you phonetically remove its first sound?

10. Rearrange each four-letter group and put it into the blanks on a single line to form an eight-letter word. The letters you insert will spell out something appropriate.

		APRT	BMOT	DEIL	ELRU		
C	A	_	A	C	_	_	_
_	N	_	O	_	_	N	T
S	E	_	_	_	A	_	E
_	E	G	_	_	A	T	_

7

11. Change one letter in each of these five words and then respace the result without rearranging the letters to form a phrase descriptive of a trainee.

LOOM   AVON   WHET   ITEM   HOLE

12. Insert a four-letter vehicle, one letter per square, across the middle row of this grid so that four common three-letter words are formed reading down.

E	A	S	T
B	R	I	E

13. What single letter can be inserted into each of these three words to form three new words?

O R E S   **M E R E**   **B E A N**

14. The three underlined words below are signs of the zodiac. What is the answer to the question?

FODJO SIM SX <u>AMEDID</u>, <u>VDCJMC</u> ST <u>ZNRTRC</u>

WSMC ISZ TMVTMCMIZ N VNDT SX ZODIAC?

15. Circle seven different letters in the reverse alphabet below to make a word meaning "treated unjustly." The word reads from left to right.

Z Y X W V U T S R Q P O N M L K J I H G F E D C B A

9

See answers to Test 1 (and scoring) on pages 10 through 13.

Test 1
ANSWERS

1. THRONE. All the others rearrange to form body parts: CHIN, KNEE, HEART, FINGER, STOMACH. The word THRONE forms HORNET.

2. Horns.

3. NG. The words created are: parings, ingrate, mongrel, and fringes.

4. 310 sugar cubes. Picture the sugar cubes that do not touch the box. They form a block of cubes measuring 5 by 12 by 3. There are 180 cubes *not* touching the box, so there are a total of 490 − 180 = 310 sugar cubes that touch the box.

5. Helipad. The word is formed by putting LIP inside HEAD, like this: HE(LIP)AD.

6.

7. The answer is 510.

Method 1

The next term is 2 times the previous term + 2. The missing term is $(2 \times 254) + 2 = 510$.

Method 2

Adding 2 to each term gives the doubling sequence 8, 16, 32, 64, 128, and 256. Add the term with its doubling sequence term for $254 + 256 = 510$.

Method 3

Each term of the sequence is 2 less than a power of two. The missing term is therefore $2^9 - 2 = 510$.

8. OAK, ELM, YEW, PINE, CEDAR, ELDER. The words formed are: cloakroom, helmet, eyewitness, dopiness, abecedarian, infielder.

9. OBOE phonetically beheaded becomes (violin) BOW.

10. Inserting TOMB
    spells CA<u>TOMB</u>. spells CA<u>T</u>ACO<u>MB</u>.

    Inserting IDLE
    spells <u>IN</u>D<u>OLE</u>NT.

    Inserting PART
    spells SE<u>PAR</u>A<u>T</u>E.

    Inserting RULE
    spells <u>REGULATE</u>.

11. LOW MAN ON THE
    TOTEM POLE.

12. BIKE. The words formed are:
    EBB, AIR, SKI, and TEE.

13. G. The three words formed
    are OGRES, MERGE, and
    BEGAN.

14. TAURUS. The decoded ques-
    tion reads: Which one of
    Gemini, Pisces, or Taurus
    does not represent a pair of
    things?

15. WRONGED.

12

Test 1

Scoring

15	pharaoh
13–14	scribe
10–12	pyramid laborer
7–9	mummified remains
0–6	cursed

Test 2

1. What secretive person is disguised here?

UCA NOG DVE EEN RRT

2. Fill in the blanks to form two words that are antonyms:

R U _ _ _   **U R** _ _ _

14 3. Complete the last diagram in this sequence.

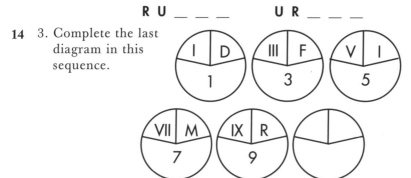

4. What 7-letter word contains the letters YZ next to each other in that order?

5. The average of 33 consecutive whole numbers is 58. What is the smallest of these whole numbers?

6. Make four men's names, each four letters long, by choosing letters from this grid.

A	R	G	O
T	I	D	E
C	A	N	T
H	O	M	E

To spell each name, choose one letter from each row, from top to bottom. It's a good idea to cross off the letters as you use them, since none of them will be used twice. What are the four names?

7. What word completes the following analogy?

ISLET is to INSOLVENT

as _____ is to PREGNANCY

8. Add the same letter 7 times to this string of letters and then respace the result to form four related words. You don't need to rearrange the letters in the string.

WLCUCKRILECNDR

9. If L B at F means "life begins at forty," then what familiar saying is this?

O of S, O of M

10. The numbers in these five diagrams combine in the same way to make correct arithmetic statements. What number is missing from the last diagram?

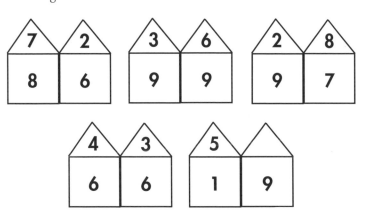

11. Rearrange the italicized word in this sentence to make a word that will fill in the blank.

> **We'll be good-naturedly *roasting* our church _____ at his retirement party.**

12. Place the 8 tiles below into the grid so that four six-letter words are formed, two reading across and two reading down.

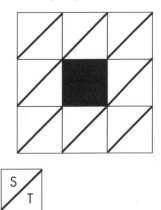

A/G E/S H/A I/T

P/R R/A R/E S/T

13. What famous city is represented here?

**(foresee − 4) + (foray − 4) + (forensics − 46)
+ (anyone − 1) + (Essex − 6)**

14. Everyone in a room writes down a two-digit number and only two people write the same number. How many people at most could be in the room?

15. Fill in a letter to complete a six-letter word reading either clockwise or counterclockwise. What is the word?

See answers to Test 2 (and scoring) on pages 20 through 23.

Test 2
ANSWERS

1. Undercover agent.
   The first letters of each letter group spell UNDER; the middle letters of each spell COVER; and the last letters of each spell AGENT.

2. RURAL and URBAN.

3. *Upper left:* consecutive odd numbers in Roman numerals.
   Bottom: same numbers in Arabic.
   Upper right: distance between letters increases by one each time.

4. Analyze.

5. 42. The average of an odd number of consecutive numbers is the middle number. Since the middle number of the 33 numbers is 58, the smallest

one is 16 numbers less than 58, which is 42.

6. Adam, Gene, Otto, Rich

7. Penny. ISLET is hidden in every second letter of I<u>N</u>S<u>O</u>L<u>V</u>E<u>N</u>T. PENNY is hidden in every second letter of <u>P</u>R<u>E</u>G<u>N</u>A<u>N</u>CY.

8. Add seven O's to form these birds: owl, cuckoo, oriole, condor.

9. Out of sight, out of mind.

10. 2. If you multiply the two triangles, you get the same answer as when you add the two squares. The calculation is $(1 + 9) \div 5 = 2$.

11. Organist.

12. This answer grid can also be flipped along the main diagonal so that AGHAST is the first word across.

13. Cannes. The words sound like letter/number combinations. You simply remove the numbers specified and use the remaining letters to spell the city as shown.

$$4C - 4 = C$$
$$4A - 4 = A$$
$$4N6 - 46 = N$$
$$NE1 - 1 = NE$$
$$S6 - 6 = S$$

14. 91. There are 90 different two-digit numbers. With one repeat, there is a maximum of 90 + 1 = 91 people in the room.

15. Casual.

Test 2

Scoring

15	champ
13–14	heavyweight
10–12	lightweight
7–9	still standing
0–6	down for the count

Test 3

1. On this number line, length PR = 14, length QS = 18 and length PS = 24. What is the length of QR?

P   Q   R   S

2. What one-word anagram of DIRTY ROOM might very well be a dirty room?

3. Enter the answers to the clues radially inward, one letter per space. The last letters of the words, already entered, will help you place the four-letter answers, which are clued in no particular order. When you are finished, the shaded area will spell a two-word phrase that you will be lucky to get.

Clues

Hard-shell dish

Profound

Pigsty sound

Religious faction

Pleasant

Repetition after a yell

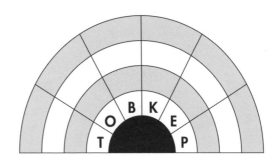

4. What world country completes this analogy?

**GLOBALIST is to INDONESIA
as KIELBASA is to _____**

5. SCRUGEAARM is "cream" and "sugar" interwoven. Both words keep their correct order from left to right. What two "this & that" words are interwoven here?

MACCHAREONEISE

6. What single letter can be inserted into each of these words to form three new words?

BRAN   SEAT   HEED

7. Mrs. Bronson pays $24 in total to buy an adult funfair ticket for herself, a student funfair ticket for her teenage son Corey, and a child funfair ticket for her younger daughter Deborah. Corey's ticket is one-third the cost of Mrs. Bronson's and Deborah's together. Also, Mrs. Bronson's ticket costs twice as much as Corey's and Deborah's tickets together. How much is each ticket?

8. Which word below is the odd one out?

**bare bore flour guerrilla
hoarse links mousse**

9. Think of a word for the first blank, and remove one letter from the
   end to form the word for the second blank. What are the two
   words?

**To create a collage involving soft, _____ colors,
I had to cut and _____ paper shapes from large sheets.**

10. At Alternative High, 99% of the 100 students are present today, but
    only 98% of the students with green hair are present. How many of
    the 100 students attending Alternative High have green hair?

11. A three-word phrase you might see on a cardboard box has been written in a row without spaces and with the vowels removed. What is this often-seen phrase?

PNTHRND

12. Add the SAME letter to each four-letter word below, and rearrange the letters to spell a five-letter word. Write the words across, one letter per square in the grid at right. The added letter must always fall in the shaded square.

ZEAL   OPEN   BOAR
GIFT   TALC

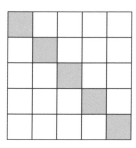

13. Listed below are 8 six-letter figures from Greek mythology in a simple substitution code. Can you crack the code and identify these beings?

YZHPZO   TBISSI   TNICJO   OMUSST

TXYZCT   OZSZCZ   MYTHIC   AHICIO

14. What are the next two numbers in the sequence below?

1 2 4 5 10 11 22 23 46 47 ___ ___

15. Insert a four-letter animal, one letter per square, across the middle row of this grid so that four common three-letter words are formed reading down.

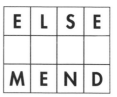

See answers to Test 3 (and scoring) on pages 30 through 33.

Test 3
ANSWERS

1. QR = 8. If PS = 24 and
   PR = 14 then RS = 10. If
   QS = 18 and RS = 10 then
   QR = 8.

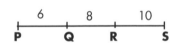

2. Dormitory.

3. The phrase is SECOND
   CHANCE.

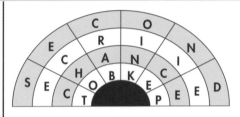

4. Italy. GLOBALIST hides
   BALI, an island of Indonesia.
   KIELBASA hides ELBA, an
   island of Italy.

5. Macaroni & cheese.

6. W. The three words formed are BRAWN, SWEAT and HEWED.

7. $16, $6, and $2. We can form these three equations:

$$B + C + D = 24$$
$$B + D = 3C$$
$$B = 2(C + D)$$

8. Flour. All of the others are homophones of animals: bear, boar, gorilla, horse, lynx, moose.

9. Pastel, paste.

10. 50 of the students attending Alternative High have green hair. Today, one student happens to be away, but this student makes up 2% of those who have green hair. Since 1 is 2% of 50, there are 50 students attending Alternative High who have green hair.

11. Open other end.

12. The added letter is H.

ZEAL	**H**	**A**	**Z**	**E**	**L**
OPEN	**P**	**H**	**O**	**N**	**E**
BOAR	**A**	**B**	**H**	**O**	**R**
GIFT	**F**	**I**	**G**	**H**	**T**
TALC	**L**	**A**	**T**	**C**	**H**

13. HERMES ATHENA
    APOLLO SELENE
    ADONIS CHARON
    SCYLLA KRONOS

14. 94 and 95. Add 1, multiply by 2, add 1, multiply by 2.

15. Lion. The words formed are: ELM, LIE, SON, END.

Test 3

Scoring

15	fine champagne
13–14	imported wine
10–12	screw top
7–9	plonk
0–6	vinegar

Test 4

1. What word completes this analogy?

   RASHEST is to TRASHES
   as MANATEE is to _____

2. Here are four views of the same block. Draw the correct top face on the final block.

3. The definitions in each row define three words. To get the next word, add an L and rearrange the letters.

For example: TINE, INLET, LENTIL

> (a) Granola morsel, saxophone range, parcel out
> (b) Second Greek letter, kitchen surface, dance form
> (c) Whispered comment, women, ventured (with "forth")

4. I have three times as much money as Amy does. If I have $26 more than Amy has, how much money do I have?

5. Add the same letter 10 times to this string of letters and then respace the result to form four related words. You don't need to rearrange the letters in the string.

L B M I N D I N L S K M I N E

6. Fill in the next domino in this sequence:

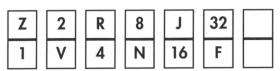

Z	2	R	8	J	32	
1	V	4	N	16	F	

7. Word Ladder: Change SHOW to BOAT, one letter at a time, in four steps. You must have a word at each step.

	S	H	O	W
	--	--	--	--
	--	--	--	--
	--	--	--	--
	B	O	A	T

8. I woke up this morning to find the hour hand of my clock pointing directly at the 38-minute mark. What time did I wake up?

9. Read these words quickly and you'll hear something you might be served in a restaurant. What is it?

balloon   gees   tressing

10. What word meaning "lie" can be represented by the word SPONSOR in a cryptogram?

11. Fill in a letter to complete a six-letter uncapitalized word. It may read either clockwise or counterclockwise. What is the word?

12. What five-letter organ of the human body becomes a different human body organ when you remove its first and last letters?

13. In each line, find a word that, when inserted, forms two phrases (such as SECOND _ _ _ _ _ _ SPLIT making "second banana" and "banana split" when BANANA is entered). The three words you supply, in order, will form a familiar phrase.

GOOSE (_ _ _) CARTON

COUGH (_ _ _ _) CLOTH

DUCK (_ _ _ _) KITCHEN

14. What four-letter word meaning "boys" becomes a word meaning "woman" when you change its last letter from an S to a Y?

15. How many times do the words PEN and INK each appear in this
grid in a straight line horizontally, vertically or diagonally?

PEN appears _____ times
INK appears _____ times

See answers to Test 4 (and scoring) on pages 40 through 43.

Test 4
ANSWERS

1. EMANATE. Move the final letter of MANATEE to the front.

2.

 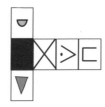

(the image on the right is the expanded block)

3. (a) oat, alto, allot.
   (b) beta, table, ballet.
   (c) aside, ladies, sallied.

4. $39.

If Amy's amount is A, then I have both 3A and A + 26.

If $3A = A + 26$, then $2A = 26$ and so $A = 13$.

If Amy has $13, then I have $39.

5. Add 10 A's to form these U.S. states: Alabama, Indiana, Alaska, Maine.

6. The letters decrease by 4, and the numbers multiply by 2.

7. S H O W
   S H O T
   S O O T
   B O O T
   B O A T

8. 7:36 A.M. If the hour hand is pointing directly at the 38-minute mark, then it is $\frac{3}{5}$ of the way between the 7 and the 8. Since $\frac{3}{5}$ of an hour is 36 minutes, the time is 7:36 A.M.

9. Blue cheese dressing.

10. UNTRUTH.

11. CASINO.

12. HEART becomes EAR.

13. The familiar phrase is egg drop soup. EGG makes "goose egg" and "egg carton"; DROP makes "cough drop" and "drop cloth"; SOUP makes "duck soup" and "soup kitchen."

14. LADS becomes LADY.

15. PEN appears 3 times and INK appears 7 times.

Test 4

Scoring

15 all-star

13–14 first stringer

10–12 second stringer

7–9 water boy

0–6 benched

Test 5

1. Five different positive whole numbers add to 30. What is the largest number that could be among the five numbers?

2. AxxxEx xxIx xUExxIOx:

   xxAx xYxE Ox AxIxAx (xxOx xExU) xxAxxx xIxx A xOUxxE xOxxOxAxx?

3. We gamble that you'll be able to figure out what these four words have in common:

SHERBET	**ASTERISK**
DOWAGER	**MISTAKE**

4. If you answer the clues and fill in the grid correctly, each letter of the alphabet will appear in the grid exactly once. We've started you off by entering the A and the Z.

Clues

"Pop" test

Odd or irrational

Logically shown to be correct

Pale yellow, as hair

Very strong

Employment office postings

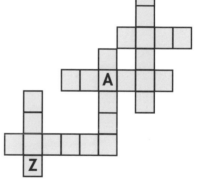

B C D E F G H I J K L M N O P Q R S T U V W X Y

5. What one-word anagram of YARD VIEW is something you might view from your yard?

6. Join the twelve fragments in this box to form four nine-letter words.

ADE	LAM	PEN	STO
INC	OGN	PSH	THO
ITO	OOM	RER	USE

7. Insert a four-letter fruit, one letter per square, across the middle row of the grid at right so that, reading down, four common three-letter words are formed.

S	H	E	D
A	W	R	Y

8. In each word of the strange-looking sentence below, every even-positioned letter has been replaced by the letter that precedes it. Can you answer the question?

WWAA WWRR FFR A MMSSCCL IISSRRMMNN WWTT A DDUULL

RREE CCNNAANN TTO PPIIS OO DDUULL LLTTEES?

9. What is the next term in this sequence?

137   106   79   56   37   22   11   ___

10. Rearrange the italicized word in this sentence to make a word that will fill in the blank.

The _____ tried to *generate* electricity
for her science fair project.

11. We hope you'll be fortunate enough to get our answer phrase when you insert letters into the blanks to form words that match the clues. What's the answer phrase?

Clues

Not hard	L A __ __ __ R
Like Dracula	C __ __ __ __ I N G
Barnyard noise	S __ __ T
Dried up	W I __ __ __ R E D
Soapy foam	V A M P __ __ __ __ __

12. Rhyme time! What do you call a university attendee who carefully saves for tuition?

13. Poison isn't nice, but can you think of three common poisons that contain the letters N, I, C, E in some order inside their names?

14. Each different letter in this multiplication question stands for a different digit. Identical letters stand for the same digit. Can you reconstruct the multiplication?

$$\begin{array}{r} \text{ADD} \\ \times\ \underline{\text{A}} \\ \text{BIT} \end{array}$$

15. What single letter can be inserted into each of these words to form three new words?

LIMO   ROOT   AIDE

See answers to Test 5 (and scoring) on pages 50 through 53.

Test 5
ANSWERS

1. 20. If the four smallest are 1, 2, 3, and 4, then they take up a total of 10 in the sum. The largest possible value for the remaining number is $30 - 10 = 20$.

2. LLAMA. Answer this question: What type of animal (from Peru) starts with a double consonant?

3. They all end in a word meaning "gamble": sherBET, asteRISK, doWAGER, miSTAKE.

4.

5. DRIVEWAY.

6. INCOGNITO, LAMPSHADE, PENTHOUSE, STOREROOM.

7. PEAR. The words formed are: SPA, HEW, EAR, DRY.

8. Bassoon. The question says, "What word for a musical instrument with a double reed contains two pairs of double letters?"

9. 4. Subtract four fewer each time. That is, subtract numbers from the sequence 31, 27, 23, 19, 15, 11, 7. The missing term is $11 - 7 = 4$.

10. Teenager.

11. The luck of the Irish.

12. A prudent student.

13. Arsenic, cyanide, strychnine.

14. $288 \times 2 = 576$. If A is larger than 3, then the answer would be more than three digits. So A = 2 or A = 3. For each of these two values, try various values of D to make the problem work.

15. B. The three words formed are LIMBO, ROBOT and ABIDE.

Test 5

Scoring

15	filet mignon
13–14	T-bone
10–12	chuck roast
7–9	rump roast
0–6	horsemeat

Test 6

1. Insert the five vowels, one of each, into the blanks to form a word.

__ N __ C __ L __ T __

2. Fill in a letter to complete a six-letter word reading either clockwise or counterclockwise. What is the word?

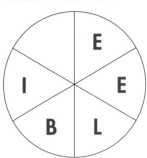

3. What do bathtubs, newlyweds, Saturn, and a tree stump have in common?

4. The numbers in the diagrams combine in the same way to make correct arithmetic statements. What number is missing from the last diagram?

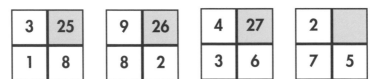

5. The word SCHEDULE has the vowel pattern EUE, since those are its vowels from left to right. Find two more single-word nouns that mean "schedule" and that have the vowel pattern AEA.

6. Place the 8 tiles into the grid so that four six-letter words are formed, two reading across and two reading down.

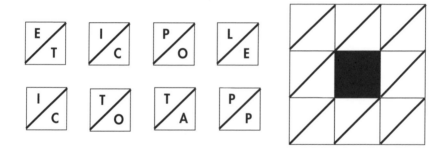

7. Use these three words to make an army member.

REID   LOST   OOF

8. The string of letters INVOERTAS is what remains when you take the Latin saying IN VINO VERITAS and remove every repeated occurrence of a letter after the first one.

What familiar saying in English results in this string, when all repeated occurrences of its letters are removed?

ALRODSETM

9. Think of a five-letter reptile. Remove the letter O and rearrange the letters to get a four-letter crustacean. What are the two animals?

10. Among 20 children who either play hockey or football (but not both), 9 play football, 8 are boys, and 8 girls are hockey players. How many boys play football?

11. Which of the choices (a), (b), (c), or (d) completes this analogy?

MASCOT is to TIE as MOTHERS is to _____

(a) fathers   (b) rest   (c) loosen   (d) cravat

12. Add the same letter 10 times to this string, and then respace the result to form four related words. You don't need to rearrange the letters in the string.

C   C   L   S   I   A   S   T   S   S   T   H   R   Z   K   I   L   G   N   S   I   S

13. It costs 25¢ to call the phone number 896-2487. Can you figure out why this would be?

14. What is the next term in the following sequence?

210   209   205   196   180   155   119   70   ___

15. Rearrange these letters to form two words that are antonyms.

NO CROP

See answers to Test 6 (and scoring) on pages 60 through 63.

Test 6
ANSWERS

1. INOCULATE.

2. EDIBLE.

3. They all have RINGS.

4. 17. Multiply the two unshaded squares on the main diagonal and then add the lower left value.

The calculation is
$(2 \times 5) + 7 = 17$.

5. AGENDA & CALENDAR.

6.

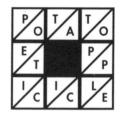

This answer grid can also be flipped along the main diagonal so that POETIC is the first word across.

7. FOOT SOLDIER.

Just read them backward with different spacing.

8. All roads lead to Rome.

9. COBRA & CRAB.

10. 5 boys play football. The information is summarized here:

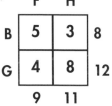

	F	H	
B	5	3	8
G	4	8	12
	9	11	

11. (b) rest. If you remove the first letter from MASCOT, you get ASCOT, defined as "tie." If you remove the first letter from MOTHERS, you get OTHERS, defined as "rest."

12. Add 10 E's to form these Bible books: Ecclesiastes, Esther, Ezekiel, Genesis.

13. Changing the numbers to their respective letters on the keypad spells TWO BITS, which is 25¢.

14. 6. Subtract the next perfect square each time. That is, subtract the numbers in the sequence 1, 4, 9, 16, 25, 36, 49, 64. The missing term is $70 - 64 = 6$.

15. PRO & CON.

Test 6

Scoring

15	Academy Award
13–14	People's Choice
10–12	rising star
7–9	character actor
0–6	extra

Test 7

1. Add as many lines as you need to transform this set of letters to a word meaning "bizarre."

CPOIFSOUL

2. What 8-letter word meaning "mention, in a way" can you create by rearranging the letters of the word MENTION around the letter A?

3. Fill in the blanks to form the only English words that have these letter patterns.

    E _ S _ G _
    E _ S _ G _ I N G

4. Insert a four-letter chemical element, one letter per square, across the middle row of this grid so that four common three-letter words are formed reading down.

A	C	H	E
D	Y	E	D

5. Fill in the two letters in each pair to make words that rhyme.
   Example: C R A N E   T R A I N.

PIE _ _   GEE _ _

SNA _ _   BRE _ _

CHE _ _   WHO _ _

6. What is the next term in this sequence?

A1 B3 E5 J7 Q9 ____

7. The three words coded below are clues to the placement of their letters in this grid. Each number in the code represents the sum of column and row headings of that letter. Can you place the letters in the proper places in the grid to spell a three-word event reading across?

	1	**2**	**3**	**4**
1				
2				
3				

3 5 7 2   6 3 4 4   4 5 5 6
B E E R   L O G O   S W A M

8. We've removed each of the five vowels from a common word. Can you reinsert those five vowels and identify the word?

D C T N

9. Five related words, each five letters long, are hidden in this grid in a continuous closed path that does not cross itself. Go from letter to letter horizontally, vertically, or diagonally. What are the five words?

R	S	T	A	C
E	T	M	R	U
L	K	C	A	T
A	I	R	E	S
U	Q	P	A	H

10. Think of a word for the first blank, and then add a letter to the front to form the word for the second blank. What are the two words?

Janice bent down a little _____ to try to grasp the stem of the _____ growing next to the gate.

11. Two 8-by-8 paper squares are laid on a table so that they overlap, forming an 8-by-11 rectangle, as shown. What is the area of the overlapping region?

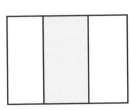

12. Insert synonyms into the blanks to make two new words.

ACCI __ __ __ **T   F** __ __ __ __

13. What single letter can be inserted into each of these words to form three new words?

D U E T   E E R Y   S H O E

14. Unscramble the topic and the list. Topic: RUNSSMITTEN.

LOCEL
BULGE
AIRGUT
CLIPCOO
NARTICLE
BEMORTON
MARCHIANO

15. I have some cookies and some small paper bags. I cannot put one cookie per bag, because there is one cookie too many for that. But I can put 3 cookies to a bag and have 5 bags left over. How many bags do I have?

See answers to Test 7 (and scoring) on pages 70 through 73.

Test 7
ANSWERS

1. **GROTESQUE**

2. NOMINATE.

3. ENSIGN & EASYGOING.

4. IRON.
   The words formed are:
   AID, CRY, HOE, END.

5. PEACE & GEESE,
   SNAKE & BREAK,
   CHEWS & WHOSE.

6. Z11. The numbers are consecutive odd numbers, and the letters increase by consecutive odd numbers.

7.

	1	2	3	4
1	R	O	S	E
2	B	O	W	L
3	G	A	M	E

8. EDUCATION.

9. Synonyms of "intelligent" in order:

ALERT

SMART

ACUTE

SHARP

QUICK

10. Lower, flower.

11. 40 square units. The height of the overlapping rectangle is 8. If the width is x, then the two remaining widths are each $8 - x$. The sum across the top is $16 - x$, which equals 11. So $x = 5$, and the area of the overlap is $5 \times 8 = 40$.

12. DEN & LAIR.
The words formed are accident and flair.

13. V. The three words thus formed are DUVET, EVERY, and SHOVE.

14. Instruments: cello, bugle, guitar, piccolo, clarinet, trombone, harmonica.

15. 8 bags.

Method 1

Solve by trial and error. The number of cookies must be a multiple of 3, so try 3, 6, 9, etc. until one works.

Method 2

If b is the number of bags, then the first statement tells us that the number of cookies is $b + 1$. The second sentence tells us that the number of cookies is $3(b - 5)$. So $b + 1 = 3(b - 5)$. Solving, $2b = 16$, so $b = 8$.

Test 7

Scoring

15   Buckingham Palace

13–14   manor house

10–12   semi-detached

7–9   hovel

0–6   cardboard box

Test 8

1. Add the same letter 5 times to this string of letters and then respace the result to form four related words. You don't need to rearrange the letters in the string.

A N B O C H E A R G O U A E A M

2. Teri's coin jar contains twice as many nickels as dimes. If the value of the dimes is $10, what is the value of the nickels?

3. Change one letter in each of the following words to make a familiar saying.

SKILL WAVERS FUN DEED

4. Fill in a letter to complete a six-letter word reading either clockwise or counterclockwise. What is the word?

5. On each line, two six-letter synonyms are woven together in order from left to right. Can you figure out the two words in each case?

C O E A A R R T S H E Y
K I I G N N I D T E L E
A N E L A R M L O S T Y

6. Think of a word for the first blank, and then remove two letters from the center to form the word for the second blank. What are the two words?

As it padded closer to the magnificent _____
horses, the cat _____ with delight.

7. Put these ten 3-letter tiles in place so that each adjacent pair of tiles forms a 6-letter word. We've already positioned LUM for you.

BAR	CUM	BIS	SCA	TAL	LUM	TRO	REN	RAB	PHY
					LUM				

8. What city in Australia can be represented by HENCHMEN in a cryptogram?

9. What letter completes the following?

C W O E U S N T T E R R Y ___

10. Rearrange the words on the left to match the clues on the right, then enter the letters across, one letter per space. The shaded columns will spell something tasty.

BEAUS						Maltreat
LEAPT						Fold
EQUIP						Excite (interest)
CLEAN						Word before corporal
AGREE						Gung-ho

11. What 6-letter word completes this analogy?

**INMATE is to INNATE
as _____ is to MATTER**

12. A woman and a man at the opera coat check receive two tags that have consecutive four-digit numbers. The sum of the digits of the lower number is 19 and the sum of the digits of the higher number is 2. What are the two tag numbers?

13. We've assigned different whole numbers to letters and then multiplied their values together to make the values of words. For example, if F = 5, O = 3, and X = 4, then FOX = 60.

Given that BIBLE = 66 and BALL = 28.
What is the value of LIBEL?

14. I'm thinking of a seven-letter word meaning "full."
The first three letters are consecutive letters of the alphabet and
the last three letters are consecutive letters of the alphabet in
reverse order. What is the word?

15. Fill in the only common word of the given length that comes
alphabetically between each of the two given words in a dictionary.

MUCH	EPOS	GLUCOSE
_ _ _ _ _ _ _	_ _ _ _ _	_ _ _ _
MUCK	EPSILON	GLUG

See answers to Test 8 (and scoring) on pages 80 through 83.

Test 8
ANSWERS

1. Add 5 D's to form these cheeses: Danbo, Cheddar, Gouda, Edam.

2. $10. There are twice as many nickels as dimes, but each nickel is worth half as much as a dime. So the nickels and dimes in the jar each total the same amount.

3. STILL WATERS RUN DEEP.

4. INFORM.

5. COARSE & EARTHY, KINDLE & IGNITE, ALMOST & NEARLY.

6. Purebred, purred.

7. The words formed, in order, are: scarab, rabbis, bistro, trophy, phylum, lumbar, barren, rental, talcum.

8. ADELAIDE.
The word has the same substitution pattern as HENCHMEN.

9. N. The words COUNTRY & WESTERN are interspersed.

10.

A	B	U	S	E
P	L	E	A	T
P	I	Q	U	E
L	A	N	C	E
E	A	G	E	R

11. MASTER.
The third letter of each word is moved one forward in the alphabet.

12. 1099 and 1100. The only four-digit numbers with a digit-sum of 2 are 2000, 1100, 1010, and 1001. The tags preceding them are 1999, 1099, 1009, and 1000, with digit-sums 28, 19, 10, and 1, respectively. Only the pair (1099, 1100) fits the situation in the question.

13. LIBEL = 132. Prime factor 28 and you get $2 \times 2 \times 7$. If BALL = $2 \times 2 \times 7$, then L = 2 and one of either B or A is equal to 1. The prime factorization of 66 is $2 \times 3 \times 11$.

If BIBLE = $2 \times 3 \times 11$, then B = 1, and since we know that L = 2, the product of I and E is 33. The value of LIBEL is the value of L × L × B × IE = $2 \times 2 \times 1 \times 33 = 132$.

14. STU<u>FFED</u>.

15. mucilage, epoxy, glue.

Test 8

Scoring

15	diva
13–14	popular singer
10–12	getting airplay
7–9	one-hit wonder
0–6	tone deaf

Test 9

1. Thaw dorw geaninm "sressed" shangec onti a dorw geaninm "ton krund" nhew uoy hwitcs sti tirsf dna tasl setterl?

2. This grid contains a two-word phrase that means "news." Start at any letter in this grid and proceed from letter to letter by moving to any adjacent letter horizontally, vertically, or diagonally. You may come back to a letter you've used previously, but may not stay in the same letter twice in a row. What is the phrase?

3. What single letter can be inserted into each of these words to form three new words?

RILE   DRAT   UNIT

4. For every three fashion magazines that I buy at the regular price, I get a fourth magazine for $1. I spent $84 for 12 fashion magazines. What is the regular price of a fashion magazine?

5. Insert a four-letter beverage, one letter per square, across the middle row of this grid so that four common three-letter words are formed reading down.

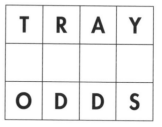

6. What is the next number in this sequence?

1 6 7 13 20 33 53 ____

7. Your job in this puzzle is to identify as quickly as you can which two letters of our alphabet are not exhibited in this very sentence.

8. Fill in the blanks to make two different things you might find in a kitchen drawer.

__ LASTIC BA __ __   __ LASTIC BA __ __

9. A three-word phrase that means "snack" has been written in a row without spaces and with the vowels removed. What is this phrase?

T B T W N M L S

10. Place the 8 tiles into the grid so that four six-letter words are formed, two reading across and two reading down.

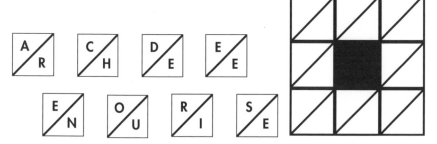

11. You're allowed to feel a little conceited if you can figure out the 9-letter word represented by these playing cards:

12. On the page opposite are three wheels. Ball A moves clockwise, one position at a time.

If ball A lands on a shaded area,
    ball B moves one place clockwise.

If ball A lands on an unshaded area,
    ball B moves two places counterclockwise.

If ball B lands on a shaded area,
    ball C moves three places counterclockwise.

If ball B lands on an unshaded area,
    ball C moves two places clockwise.